Think Positively

Inspirational Thoughts
For Each and Every Day

Think Positively

*Inspirational Thoughts
For Each and Every Day*

*Edited by
Jesse Sposato*

Wild Poodle Books
New York

Think Positively:
Inspirational Thoughts For Each and Every Day

Edited by Jesse Sposato

Cover Illustration by J. Longo

Illustrations by Jessica Dowling

For complete information regarding individual poems, please see
page 61

Published by
Mud Puddle Books, Inc.
54 W. 21st Street
Suite 601
New York, NY 10010
info@mudpuddlebooks.com

ISBN: 978-1-60311-156-0

Interior design and layout by Michelle Gengaro

Printed in Singapore

Contents

Keys to Happiness

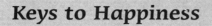

Take time to smell the flowers;
enjoy the sun upon your face.
Celebrate life to its fullest
as if you might soon leave this place.

Treasure always your loved ones,
treat every person as a friend,
be kind to all living things;
only good thoughts should you send.

Reflect, don't dwell on the past;
live in the present all you can.
Look ahead to the future and
take hold of life with both hands.

Never lose sight of your dreams,
stay young at heart and mind,
always help those in need,
and true happiness you will find.

—By Jennifer Parks-Nolan

Graceful Celebration

*Today is a graceful celebration with shiny
sunny skies, sparkling, glistening, gleaming.*

*The celebration is in the company that we keep,
the mood we meet in the morning.*

*Today is a graceful celebration, angels flying in
the sky.*

*Today is a graceful celebration, fireworks going
off in the twilight.*

Today is a graceful celebration.

—By Kimberly Strothman Anderson

Breathing Beauty

Just breathing is beautiful,
even when mirrors break,
or when your hands don't fit
or when you're planning your escape.

Just living is love,
even when your heart is chipped,
or when you love someone dearly,
and they don't respond near to it.

Just flying is freedom,
even when your wing is dull,
or when you can't find the courage
to do what you love.

And when I can't find the air,
I'll still fight off these demons,
because my heart is love,
where beauty is breathing.

—By Taylor Flynn

A Clear, Bright Star

Looking at the night sky
I search for a clear, bright star
To relay how much I miss you
And how dearly loved you are

I send up to it a kiss goodnight
And a wish for dreams so sweet
A warm embrace that fills your heart
Until it makes you feel complete

I send up my faith in all you do
To keep you strong within
And a cheerful smile
So sadness never can set in

I send up to it my heart and soul
So you'll never feel alone
With a prayer
You will be safe and sound
And that you'll soon be home

I send up my fervent wish
That you'll know my love is true
And when you see a clear, bright star
You'll know what it holds for you

—By Lynn C. Johnston

Awakening

Every day is an awakening.
Smother the sun in my desires.
Recognize the potential;
Ignore the negative. Your world
is your positive.
Your thoughts are your logic.
What you desire is your fire, and
the burn is endless.
You lay on it..success is equivalent.
Mentally. Emotional. Love; How?
Give me peace.
This moment; questions me.
test my faith in my resolve for a better me.
All negative influences; are beyond my need.
I hear you, and I still know better.
A passion for more; is the driver.
I want more.

—By Keisha DeBarros

The Hereafter

to be a scent or a memory
to leave a vision of your face
the sound of your soft voice
to matter in this world.

to fill a small space in this universe
to be of interest to another
to have mattered to someone at birth
to have mattered as something at death.

—*By Jean Roland*

New Days

Everyday the sun shines down,
To find you asleep in your bed.
Awake to the light of the brand new day,
Let hope inspire your head.
Up off the pillow of worried dreams,
And into the room of survival.
Your night has washed away your past,
New morning brings revival.
Though times are getting worse by days,
And reason more scarce to find.
We know that what we have in the end,
Is that which fills our mind.
Be it love, or hate, or anger,
Patience, dreams or ideas.
We cannot trade what we wish,
For all we know that is.
And if ever you struggle to find,
A light to bathe your soul,

Look no further than your own two hands,
For it, is all in your control.
We take the bad we learn,
We allow it to help us grow strong,
The minutes pass as we continue,
The days won't seem so long.
So please awake, rise your head,
Go strong into the day,
Let love and hope be inspiration,
To guide you on your way.
The time is now, the sun is up,
Allow warmth your soul to take,
And worry not for life is long,
A new morning is here,
My friend.
Awake.

—By Michael Orlando

Oceans Of Love

I walked along the sands of time,
Near the water's edge life defined,
Storms that raged in a haggard Soul
Sprays that whispered of more to know.
I picked up shells along the way,
Saving them for a rainy day,
Shells of laughter, of joy and love,
Still somehow it was not enough.
The message was clear, 'Go Within,
Shells to find where beginning ends.'
Tides of senses to become whole,
Ebbing and flowing, touching Soul.
Oceans of love from God above,
Drenched in it's spray, washed in his love.

—By Catherine Lindsey

Eloquent Manifestation

How I love thee
Beauty in the sky
Rainbows in the moonlight
Eloquent understanding
Brush of love
How I love thee
Sunset on the water
Ice cream in the springtime
Joy during the harvest
How I love thee
Friendship blossoms

—By Kimberly Strothman Anderson

Roaring Silence

Have you ever mistaken a shooting star for a firefly?
Have you ever had a whale look you in the eye?
Have you ever let a baby see you cry?

Find those moments when clouds fly by
In Roaring Silence as you look to the Sky.

—By Jaime Warner

A Tally Mark

Every smile, every laugh
Leaves a tally mark behind
A residue of happiness
Enriching a heart and mind
Every loving gaze
Brings solace to the soul
Leaving peace and quiet
When fear's been in control
Every sympathetic ear
And every caring touch
Lingers in the spirit
To provide a needed crutch
Even a brief moment
Can become a special gift
A memory we can treasure
That will comfort and uplift
But if that moment is forgotten
And never brought to mind
It still touched a life with kindness
Leaving a tally mark behind

—By Lynn C. Johnston

Truly Blessed

When I found more pain in others
Than I found within myself
I learned what it meant to feel compassion
And my pain began to fade

When I found more forgiveness in others
Than I found within myself
I learned what it meant to feel peace
And my heart began to mend

When I found more belief in others
Than I found within myself
I learned what it meant to have faith
And my fears began to die

And when I found more love in others
Than I found within myself
I learned what it meant to feel truly blessed
And my spirit began to soar

—By Lynn C. Johnston

Life is short

Life is short and it should be appreciated.
Each day we have should be celebrated.
Life is short because time flies.
It's a fact that it doesn't take long for the years to
   pass by.
Before we know it, a whole lifetime has passed.
We should make the most of life because time
   goes by so fast.

—By Randy Johnson

I Believe

I believe
In the positive forces
Of the universe
And supplicate them everyday
That they may help me
Walk toward the light
Giving and receiving
Love, joy and wisdom.
I pray the same for all of us.

I believe
In everlasting love;
And that once we have found
Our Heart's Desire
We will never be alone again;
But always faithfully companioned
Through each pristine blush of spring,
Searing sun of summer,
Sanguine sojourn of autumn,
And bitter frost of winter;

Taking comfort in the knowledge
That life always renews itself.
I hope you believe that as well.

I believe
In the indomitable human spirit;
That we can accept
Without succumbing
Relinquish, to embrace the unknown;
Battle, with grace and dignity
And trust in the triumph of our own goodness.
May your faith be just that strong.

And I believe in humankind;
That we are intelligent, talented,
Kind souls who take little and give much
So may those positive forces of which I speak
Be with us and bless forever.
Amen

—By Karen R. Springer

Share Joy!

See the smile of a little boy,
playing with his favorite toy.
Hear him giggle with glee.
This is how we used to be!
When did we forget to wonder at the sunrise?
Or raise our voices in righteousness?
If only we could learn to live for today.
Take next to nothing and run away!
Watch the sunrise and set with only sustenance to
  bear.
Think how much we'd have if only we all could share!

—By Nina Size

Shadow Dancing

We are shadows dancing,
a sigh left on the breeze,
we are sweet inspiration,
which drags us to our knees.

We are shadows dancing,
playing in candlelight,
we are light refracting
on gooseflesh milky white.

We are shadows dancing,
a long, drawn out slow dance,
lovers in the making,,
clay in the palm of a hand.

We are shadows dancing,
upon the face of the moon,
we are tunes for singing,
lovers in a swoon.

We are shadows dancing,
playing upon the wind,
sweet and comely inspiration,
come on, let's do it again.

—By Catherine Lindsey

A Privilege

It is a privilege
To have awaken up this morning.
Others did not make it.
It is a privilege
To go to work this morning.
Others have no work place to go.
It is a privilege
To kiss someone for good-bye
When you leave your house
Some leave nobody behind
The door to wait for them.
It is a privilege
To have dinner with someone
And even to wash the dishes
For your family
Some have no other dishes to wash.

It is a privilege
To hear the telephone ringing,
Some pay the telephone bill
For years and nobody calls.
It is a privilege
To go out with a friend,
Some are never invited
Or have nobody to invite.
It is a privilege
To be kissed, hugged, touched
Loved or wanted.
Some only long for these.
It is a privilege
To be a parent
No matter how hard it may be,
And how many sleepless nights
This may cause.
Some only hope to be needed.

It is a privilege
To grow wise and old,
To be someone's grandparent
Or mentor,
Some never share this
Unique and fascinating
Time of returning
To innocence.
It is a privilege
Having someone to take away
The blanket from you
Or silently breath
On the second pillow.
Some can't share the blanket
At all.
It is a privilege
Having someone in your life
To long for your caress,
For your look and attention
For an "I love you".
Some have nobody to
Tell this magic to.

It is a privilege
To be asked for a favour,
Some don't enjoy this feeling
Of being needed
Admired or helpful
It is a privilege,
All this routine,
All these small things we are doing
For us or for others.
Some are not this blessed anymore.
It is a privilege
Even being able to read now
These lines.
Some can only read with their
Fingers.

—By Adria Martin

My Guardian Angel

Whenever there's something upsetting or frightening
Echoing thunder, crackling lightening,
Shadows that startle and spiders that crawl,
People who make me feel silly and small,
Duties I'm not sure I'm ready to shoulder
That just seem to multiply as I get older,
The fear that I'll fail and the fear of rejection,
Or anything else from which I need protection,
With strong arms and wise words, you're always there
To fight off the bad things that threaten and scare.
So bugs, fears, and thunder, you'd better watch out,
Or my guardian angel will knock you right out!

—By Rachel Tornheim

Life: Scene 1, Take 1

*Life is full of adversity; choices and decisions we make
daily.
Each decision and choice leads us down a different
road in life.
One road may be full of love, good fortune, and
prosperity,
While the other might be full of depression,
loneliness, and despair.
We decide our own fate upon each decision being
made,
Although we never fully know the outcomes and
consequences of each.
Life is a roller coaster of emotions, feelings, and
thoughts,*

The high point being our happiest moments,
While the low being our saddest.
But in life we will never remain stagnant at the
    peak of the roller coaster,
Nor shall we dwell in the valley either.
Life is each day waking up and realizing that this
    particular day,
Is the most important day of our life.
Life is love and hate, happiness and sadness,
    confusion and curiosity.
Life is never always great, and life is never always
    terrible.
Life happens, life is life.

—By Christopher Cella

My Millennium Wish

*As I look back at the past, I'm amazed at what
    we've done
We've put men on the moon and the computer age
    has begun
Automobiles in every garage, TVs in each home
Fax machines and VCRs, compact discs and mobile
    phones*

*We've seen the best man has to give through
    nature's adversity
But we've also seen man's evil side; his cruel
    inhumanity
With the bomb, we've learned to kill those we've
    never seen
We hunted and killed the innocent to fulfill our evil
    schemes*

*We judged those who were different by birth or just
    by choice
We freely scorned not knowing them or listening to
    their voice
We no longer know our neighbors and we've lost
    track of faithful friends
Guns and knives have replaced our words, violent
    means to deadly ends*

My millennium wish is to focus on the people in this
    world
Let's put aside our judgments and embrace each boy
    and girl
Instead of seeing differences and all that could divide
Let's look for commonality throughout this world so
    wide

Let's reach out to our neighbors and the sick and
    elderly
Let's make sure every child's loved, living happy and
    carefree
Let's make this world a cleaner place without
    pollution or disease
Let's not have to worry about what's in our air and
    in our seas

Let's value people over money and make sure
    everyone is fed
Let's see they have a warm, safe place and a strong
    roof over their head
Let's try to leave this world a little better than it was
And hope the next millennium will have more
    compassion and more love

    —By Lynn C. Johnston

Remember

As life passes us by, remember to wave
to the memories, to everything that we gave
to the all the times you told yourself "I won't
    quit"
When faith stepped in and rerouted your ship
When you got off path, and got off course
When you finally crashed and had to swim to the
    shore

When relatives passed away, and you passed out
When the sun once shined only to get choked by
    clouds
When the love that you held so high, fails
When the train you were riding becomes derailed

Don't bail at the first sight of danger
Hold your head high in the face of a stranger
Speak your voice, fight to be heard
You have lived your life, rejoice, and remember

every word

That you spoke, every thought you ever dreamed
Remember that fear and the sound of every
  scream
Remember that pain, and how you overcame
the obstacles in your life, and now you still
  remain

Through it all you stood tall, and your heart was
  always true
And for the life you live, may the gods watch over
  you

—By Corey Grant

Young At Heart

May I always be young at heart
falling backwards into the autumn leaves
dancing on the edges of reality
welcoming life like a cool breeze.
May I always jump from the loft
into a pile of hay
breathe deep the flower's fragrance
and sit in awe as the lights
are reflected upon the bay.
May I always giggle with the girls
and cry for the child inside
feel the pain of another's suffering
and soar with the eagles on high.
May I always embrace a friend
shed a tear upon goodbye
filled with love, and light, and laughter
while reaching for the sky.
and when called upon, may I do my part
yes, may I always be
young at heart.

—By Catherine Lindsey

A Song Of Music In Daily Life

We weave the chords of music in our daily lives;
the harp, the flute, the piano, the drums.
My friend and I are bound
together by my neighbor's vast
supply of classical music that
we listen to as
we sit out on the patio. Each certain
string, each chord he plays
has a different tune.

We share a cup of green mint tea as the flute player
next door practices
a last minute piece for his midnight recital.

We'd love to hear him play at a real concert
but his show has already sold
out.
There are no more tickets. But that doesn't
matter; here, underneath the leaves of a tall
sycamore,
we have front row seats.

—By Apryl Fox

The Source of Hope

There are many signs and wonders when you look
   around
Of the source of hope that is waiting to be found –

The vibrant, lustrous beauty of a fresh spring flower,
The nourishing refreshment of a gentle rain shower,

The song of a robin when it wants to speak,
The majesty of a snow-covered mountain peak,

The warmth of the sun shedding its light,
The pattern of stars in the sky at night,

The rainbow that appears following the rain,
The nutrition that's provided by a field of grain.

In our lives we can find the source of hope too,
No matter what circumstances we are going through –

In sickness and pain, disappointment or grief,
We can have hope that we will find relief.

God is the source of hope for us all
And will bring us comfort when on him we call.

God pierces the darkness with the light of love
And gives us the peace that comes from above,

Then we can rejoice in our hearts and sing,
Giving praise to God for every good thing.

—By Connie Arnold

Circle Of Friends

At Some Point In Our Lives We Find
Special People That We Can Call Our Friends,
They Will Be There To Guide Us In Hard Times
And Will Help Our Hearts To Mend.

Our Circle Of Friends Are There When Needed
And They Will Help Us Dry Our Tears,
And Also When We Get Frightened
They Will Calm Us From All Our Fears.

It's Comforting To Know We Belong
And On Each Other We Can Depend,
We Will Be There For One Another
In Our Special Circle Of Friends.

—By Melinda Tanner

Small Favors

It's like miracles in movement as I lay here with you
The pleasure and your adornment to me is like a
    dream come true
I often wonder how I was chosen to be
such a worthy ally for only my treasured eyes to see
But I don't ponder too much on that, I just thank
    the universe for the small favors that are thrown
    my way
And I pray that I get to exist in your world for
    another day.

Memories flow in and out of my mind with the
    countless times you've made my heart smile
I am warmed by your presence, your essence, your
    gift, your love
So I thank the universe for the small favors that
    are sent down from the heavens above

      —By Keith Givens

What if...

Each day goes by and I wonder what if...

What if...I flew that kite
What if...I took time to watch that rainbow
   disappear
What if...the bubbles didn't burst or
reflections
   in the water stayed til the end of time
What if...

What if...the beautiful blue sky with clouds
   stayed or the horizon falling over the ocean
   or the moon on the lake stayed.
What if...

I would find the embrace of beauty.

Beauty is with us. Let's embrace it.

—Kimberly Strothman Anderson

The power of a hug

When my soul slowly gets back
Into my sleepy body,
After a night of journey
In the land of dreams,
While my eyes are still closed,
I think of a reason to wake up
Something to make me wish
To get down from the bed.
And I really can't,
I can't find any better reason
Than an imaginary hug
To give me strength,
To give me the confidence,
The love, the hope,
And the joy to live,
In confidence
The gift of
Another day.

—By Adria Martin

Words Spoken In Anger

Sticks And Stones May Break My Bones
But Words Will Never Hurt Me
For Some This Is True
For Others Sorrow Moans
And Leaves Open Wounds For All To See
Don't Say Cruel Words In Anger
That You May Not Even Mean
Because Each Word Used
Leaves The Danger
Of Hurt You Can Never Redeem
Don't Laugh And Snicker
Poke Fun Or Cause Fear
Because If You Cause A Bicker
It's Not Worth Your Victim's Tear
Look Around As Your Words Grow
Where Your Friends Were Last
And Watch The Stones You Throw
Turn Your House To Glass

—By Teresa Bright

44

Raining On The Ocean

It is raining on the ocean.
Not because I am king,
and I wear a crown,
or because I dance my way
to the ocean's gods,
or because I have sold my soul
to buy a better one.
It is raining on the ocean.
Not because I have failed,
and lost my way,
or because the mountain is too steep
to climb and build
or because you are not here with me.
It is raining on the ocean
to wake me up,
and to remember that I am flesh,
I am blood,
and there is no greater feeling
on this earth of mine,
then knowing it is raining on the ocean
because I am alive.

—By Taylor Flynn

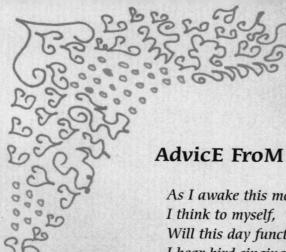

AdvicE FroM EartH...

As I awake this morning
I think to myself,
Will this day function??
I hear bird singing as cars go by.
Watching the earth rotate,
as I sit in one place...
Today speaks to me,
giving me advice,
to be strong,
just move along...

Knowing that the earth loves me,
is the most beautiful part of this day...
The earth is telling me,
"Nicholas,"
decrease all that negative energy,
increase....
Increase your care for others,
show your friends and brother,
what we can all do for each other.....

THANK YOU EARTH,
for the advice of a wise man,
giving out a hand,
to see things in a different circumstance.
Telling me from what's right and wrong.

To you earth,
I'll always be strong....
As strong as your mountains,
valleys,
rivers,
oceans,
and trees.
I know, beautiful earth, you're here for me...
I will always believe.

—By Nicholas A.

Untitled

Some often let the grains of sand
slip through their grasp with ease
untouched they 'scape their folded hands
like wind passing through trees
So small the grains some cannot catch
and beaten is the way
the path fools take which leads them straight
and never twists nor strays
So wander if you are not lost
and take the ragged trail
hold fast the grains and look ahead
to mountains you can scale

—By Teressa Walsh

48

Grace

Touch my cheek with the brush of your hand,
kiss my lips and sigh,
whisper love notes to me all night long,
sing a tender lull-a-bye.

Touch my heart with your words,
set my soul aflame,
tell me this night will never end,
softly call my name.

Take my hand and draw me near,
in a warm embrace,
hold on tight to my trembling heart,
fill me with grace.

—By Catherine Lindsey

Slow Down

The world is turning fast about me
And in it rushing and stress is all I see,
People spend their days waiting for night,
While the darkness is spent waiting for light.
Don't people see it's time to stop and look around,
Then they could see what I've already found.
Understand that all you'll ever have is just today,
And waiting for tomorrow just wastes it away.
So prepare for the future but enjoy the present;
For if life is anything, it is just this moment.

—By Mohammed Kaleel

The Night

Darkness drifts gently o'er the town
Slowly washing the daylight away
Streetlights illuminate a barren sidewalk
As it comes to the close of the day

A story before bedtime
Or a cup of chamomile tea
Inviting weary souls to rest
Daytime sounds begin to fade
While a baby slumbers on daddy's chest

Lovers bathe in a full moon's glow
Stars twinkle brightly up above
As countless wishes are sent up
By those in search of love

Tomorrow's just a fantasy
'Til sunlight burns the night away
Birds chirp rejoicing
Another dawning of a day

—By Lynn C. Johnston

Inspirer

There's a fire, burning in your eyes,
and from within an inspiration lies...
And cries, and tries, to be undone-
composing raptures for my one.
And each note could not be made,
if not for feelings you persuade.
You coax them from my very soul.
Rise them up and extol,
the essence of a love so true,
that everyday is bright and new!

—By Nina Size

The Meaning Of Friendship

Your Friendship Means The World To Me
More Than Words Can Ever Say,
As We Continue To Grow Closer Together
More With Each Passing Day.

Your Friendship Being Like A Flower
Petals Glistening In The Morning Dew,
Your Friendship Started A New Beginning For Me
And A Way Of Life Brand New.

Your Friendship Is Like A Treasure Chest
Filled With Gems And Purest Gold,
I Am Thankful That I Now Have You
And Together We'll Grow Old.

Thanks For Your Friendship!

—By Melinda Tanner

Your Way

I know everything won't always go your way
Sometimes you might wake up and feel like it's just
*   not your day*
But you must remember all there is to be thankful
*   for*
Friends, family, dreams and more

So, on days when you wake up on the wrong side of
*   the bed*
Try to make it better, even if only in your head

Tomorrow is always full of hope
Tomorrow is always full of promise

But today is right now
So let the world be on your side

Put everything you've got into making it good
Because at least you'll know you've tried
At least you'll know you could!

—By Mandy Kerrigan

Peace

There is peace running through
the alcoves of my mind
like a lazy river meandering on
caring nothing about time.

There is peace in my days and nights
each so separate and on its own
filled with peace and happiness
each aspect stands alone.

There is peace resting there
on the outskirts of my life
where tiny lees in a pool
ripple but once or twice.

—By Catherine Lindsey

Ever Since

Ever since you entered my life
I see the sun brighter

I like your heart
And how it is so encouraging

Being with you
Makes me appreciate life

If only every person
On this Earth

Would take the time
To appreciate that person in their lives

Don't take them for granted
Take the time to see what you have

Ever Since
You entered my life

My eyes have opened
And I have seen

How blessed that I am with you
You have truly changed me

Like no other person
On this Earth ever has

Every moment that I am with you
Feels like a walk in the clouds

Ever since you entered my life
My heart has beat faster

I am so incomplete without you
You are truly my other half

My hearts beats
When yours does

My soul feels brighter
When it's near your soul

Ever since you came into my life
I have become complete

—By Erik Herrera

You only live once

You only live once so don't spend your life being
depressed.
You are a fantastic human being and that makes
you blessed.
Please don't feel sorry for yourself or think negative
thoughts.
Be filled with joy because of the friends and family
you've got.
Don't beat yourself up because of the wrong things
you've done.
You are a very special person so kick up your heels
and have fun.
You shouldn't feel bad because of your flaws,
everybody else has flaws too.
Just do good things and treat people with respect,
that's all you have to do.

—By Randy Johnson

Brightening

the sun leaks around the edges of the
window shade eclipsing the night-ness
of the room, the warm orange glow eats
at the shadows that haunt the blackness
of dreams, the bleak cold of the room is
challenged by the radiant raider, the body
stirs, the terrors of the night give way
to new fantasies, the brightening spirit
takes hold and welcomes life with love.

—By Jean Roland

Memories

Yesterday is far away, to never be lived again
Today is the day, all new memories begin
So live life today
For tomorrow today will be far away

—By Jaime Warner

Think Positively
Inspirational Thoughts For Each and Every Day

Acknowledgements

Keys to Happiness
Jennifer Parks-Nolan
Copyright © 2008 by Jennifer Parks-Nolan
Used by permission of the author

Graceful Celebration
Kimberly Strothman Anderson
Copyright © 2008 by Kimberly Strothman Anderson
Used by permission of the author

Breathing Beauty
Taylor Flynn
Copyright © 2008 by Taylor Flynn
Used by permission of the author

A Clear, Bright Star
Lynn C. Johnston
Copyright © by Lynn C. Johnston (www.lynncjohnston.com)
First published in Angel's Dance: A Collection of Uplifting & Inspirational Poetry by
Lynn C. Johnston; Published: 2006
Used by permission of the author

Awakening
Keisha DeBarros
Copyright © 2008 by Keisha DeBarros
Used by permission of the author

The Hereafter
Jean Roland
Copyright © 2008 by Jean Roland
Used by permission of the author

New Days
Michael Orlando
Copyright © 2008 by Michael Orlando
Used by permission of the author

Oceans Of Love
Catherine Lindsey
Copyright © 2008 by Catherine Lindsey
Used by permission of the author

Eloquent Manifestation
Kimberly Strothman Anderson
Copyright © 2008 by Kimberly Strothman Anderson
Used by permission of the author

Roaring Silence
Jaime Warner
Copyright © 2008 by Jaime Warner
Used by permission of the author

A Tally Mark
Lynn C. Johnston
Copyright © by Lynn C. Johnston (www.lynncjohnston.com)
First published in Angel's Dance: A Collection of Uplifting & Inspirational Poetry by
Lynn C. Johnston; Published: 2006
Used by permission of the author

Truly Blessed
Lynn C. Johnston
Copyright © by Lynn C. Johnston (www.lynncjohnston.com)
First published in Angel's Dance: A Collection of Uplifting & Inspirational Poetry by
Lynn C. Johnston; Published: 2006
Used by permission of the author

Life is short
Randy Johnson
Copyright © 2008 by Randy Johnson
Used by permission of the author

I Believe
Karen R. Springer
Copyright © 2008 by Karen R. Springer
Used by permission of the author